THE BRIDAL COMPANY

The Bridal Company:

Copyright © 2020 Brian Guerin

All rights reserved. No part of this book may be used or reproduced by any means, graphic, electronic, mechanical, including photocopying, recording, taping, or by any information storage retrieval system without the written permission of the author except in the case of brief quotations embodied in critical articles and reviews.

Scripture quotations taken from the New American Standard Bible® (NASB), Copyright © 1960, 1962, 1963, 1968, 1971, 1972, 1973, 1975, 1977, 1995 by The Lockman Foundation Used by permission. www.Lockman.org

ISBN: 9798695293555

*Cover design, typeset, & development by *Tall Pine Books*

|| Printed in the United States of America

THE BRIDAL COMPANY

BRIAN GUERIN

BridalGlory.com

CONTENTS

Introduction   vii

PART I
THE BRIDAL CALL

1. The Bridegroom in My Ministry   3
2. Bridal Encounters   7
3. All Roads Lead to the Bridegroom   11
4. The Knocking of the Bridegroom   15
5. Foundations of The Bridal Company   19

PART II
BRIDAL GRACE, WORKS, & REWARDS

6. The Bridal Company Distinction   27
7. Empowered by Grace   31
8. Yielding to the Bridegroom   35
9. Heavenly Rewards   41
10. Parable of the Bridesmaids   47

PART III
A BRIDE MADE READY

11. Closeness with the Bridegroom   53
12. Ingredients of the Bridal Company: Purity   57
13. Ingredients of the Bridal Company: Intimacy   65
14. Ingredients of the Bridal Company: Obedience   75
15. Bridal Union   79

ABOUT THE AUTHOR   85
FREE EXCERPT FROM CONTEMPLATIONS ON CHARACTER   89
Notes   99

INTRODUCTION

I would like to lay a foundation to undergird the revelation you will receive throughout this book. I believe this will be truest to form as a reflection of who we are as a ministry. In the coming chapters, I set out to explain the insight of the Bridal Realm by including a combination of the Word, Spirit, and a whole lot of Jesus. *The Bridal Company* represents our core values as a ministry and my desire for Jesus to deeply touch you and draw you into union with Him.

I believe the heartbeat of God is honing in this hour. I've been able to tap into different things by his Spirit such as dreams, visions, angelic encounters, heavenly visitations and more. However to date, nothing has come close to my experiences with the Lord *as Bridegroom*. In this book, we will get into some of those dreams, visitations, and prophecies but it all connects back to the Bridal company that we feel called to raise up.

The Theme of the Bridal Message is Intimacy

Throughout the book, you will see a constant theme. The theme is the message of *intimacy*. No matter what the subject, you will always see us coming back to union with Jesus Christ. Some people are not as 'deep' as others and that's okay because in this book it will be all about you being drawn as His bride. From this place, I intend to build and go forth into deeper revelation.

I am very excited about this work. From the beginning, we have been consumed with this bridal message and raising up a bridal company. As you go about this journey, I hope and pray you can feel God's heart concerning the message of the Bridegroom. The Bridegroom wants to hand out bridal assignments from a place of intimacy. Even if you are not familiar with bridal lingo, the encounters, scriptural references, communion with Jesus will bring you to full revelation of Jesus as Bridegroom; as well as an understanding of your identity as His Bride. Jesus, our bridegroom, is raising up a fellowship that is beyond terminology. Are you ready to be a part of this last day bridal company?

My Prayer Concerning You

My prayer is that Jesus would be glorified in this teaching. I pray that He would wreck your world with the revelation of Himself as the Bridegroom. I ask that He would throw new mantles upon you of intimacy like never before. Let your heart be melted into oneness with Him and let his Word come alive in you. I pray The Spirit breathes fresh wind and shows you His glory so that you may know Him in a deeper way. May the Lord take precedence, wreck your world, and cloak you in his closeness. As you read this book, may wonders appear in your life, that God may be glorified.

PART I

THE BRIDAL CALL

1. THE BRIDEGROOM IN MY MINISTRY

I want to share with you the testimony of my call into the bridal realm and the beginning of our ministry *Bridal Glory International*. I pray that as you read our start, your world would be wrecked with the revelation of Jesus Himself as the Bridegroom. May the Spirit breathe fresh wind and show you His glory so that you may know Him in a deeper way. I first heard the call to follow the bridegroom at the age of 20 years old on September 23, 1998. After I met Jesus Christ, I fell completely in love with Him.

I was consumed with intimacy with Jesus. Our ministry did not actually start until 2010-2011. This is important for you to know. If you do the math, this equals a 12 to 13 year gap in which I was waiting, with deep intimacy, on the Bridegroom. In the scriptures, the apostle Paul had a similar gap of 14 years of waiting on the Lord. During this gap, like Paul, I had been ministering but hadn't officially started the ministry.

Somewhere in that gap, there was a building pocket

consisting of a series of events. During this season of being with the Lord, I went to Brownsville Revival Bible College for two years. It was a powerful AG church. I remained there until 2004. The revival that took place there greatly impacted me as I learned so much. That time also launched me into many encounters, even greater intimacy, and our current ministry—*Bridal Glory International.*

Many wonder about that name, *Bridal Glory International,* and how it was birthed. Our name was not just something I sat and thought up. Rather, our name as a ministry was held before the Lord. One time, I had a funny experience at an airport in which a woman was confused concerning our name Bridal Glory. She confused the name of our ministry with a women's show about wedding dresses. I laughed but did not correct her. For me, the name of our ministry is very important. It was birthed through a supernatural vision and it speaks to our mission as a ministry.

The greater underlying theme that God has us doing as a ministry can be summed up as follows: we are dedicated to the ever evolving of becoming His beloved bride ourselves; while calling in and preparing the bride worldwide for the culmination of all things and becoming one with Him. This is what I believe He is doing. There's a bridal company He's raising up that's beyond lingo. You can feel God's heart, with the revelation of the bridegroom, and His desire to raise up a bridal company throughout the earth.

The Bridal Message

Many wonder about the miracles, visions, dreams, and prophetic encounters that mark our ministry. This all flowed out of that gap season and an encounter I had with a falcon after which the prophetic exploded in my life. Much of what we do today as a ministry, was birthed from this falcon encounter. There was also a series of other encounters that followed that transformed my world. The call to the bridegroom is our message out of all these experiences. This message, that was formed in those seasons, has forever wrecked me. It is our primary message and is our greatest priority. I am big on the need to preach the full gospel message; souls, healing, teaching, prophetic, and the apostolic. I love it all. We are big on it all. We love these other messages especially the prophetic ones. Our very first school that came out of this deep bridal intimacy was a school of the prophetic. As much as we love these other topics, the *bridal* message has become the main focus.

    I really can't change the subject or see anything else. Every other message became secondary to me. I am undone by the revelation of Jesus as the bridegroom and I hope you become undone as well. Although we do a lot of different things, our theme as a ministry is always coming through the tunnel of intimacy, infatuation with the Lord, and purity. So don't get me wrong we love it all and we try to do it all. But I will forever see life through the bridal realm and intimacy with Jesus.

2. BRIDAL ENCOUNTERS

Many times, God will set up divine 'tie-ins' to your call. Divine tie-ins are prophetic moments that propel you into greater understanding of your call and identity in Him. They linger with you for the rest of your life. Anything you tap into prophetically is forever obtainable. That is why seers and seeing in the spirit is so powerful.

The seer company is greatly needed in the last days. In Revelation 3:8, the church was told to anoint her eyes so that she could see. In chapter 4, the bible mentions how the fourth head on the living creature was the eagle in flight. The eagle represents seeing in the prophetic. Joel 2 prophecies about the increase in revelation in the last days. The book of Joel says that God will pour out his spirit on all flesh but also mentions dreams, visions, prophecy and signs & wonders. These are all revelatory. Before the day of pentecost, Jesus told the disciples to wait for power from on high. Jesus's description of the Holy Ghost coming is *power*. Joel prophesied revelatory manifestations of the spirit, while Jesus spoke of a power demonstration of the spirit—but they were both concerning the Spirit.

Seven years after the falcon encounter, I experienced another encounter. We had just gotten started into the prophetic lane. I went on a forty day fast led by the Lord. I completed this fast with a buddy of mine—it was a God fast, with twenty one days of Daniel fast and a nineteen day liquid fast. I encountered what I call the "light vision." The forty day fast opened up this particular vision.

The Lord totally interrupted the conversation I was having with my friend in California right at noon with the same experience of Paul. I was in California and when it occurred, I had a vision in which Jesus blinded me with the light at 12:01. Paul had a light encounter himself and retells the account to King Agrippa. He tells the king it was about *noon* that day and a blinding light came out of heaven. I said, "Oh my goodness, the Lord was mimicking my encounter to that of Paul's." It was a parallel encounter, allowing me to know my assignments.

Jesus said to Paul, out of the blinding light, "Why do you persecute me?" and right there a commissioning happened. I had also felt a commission. I was then thrust into a season in which I encountered the cloud of witnesses. I saw Paul, from the cloud of witnesses, laying in my bed. As this would happen, I noticed the veil became very thin. The bed is a symbol of intimacy. I believe this represented intimacy with the Lord just as Paul had. These bridal encounters became the intimate foundation of the ministry God was calling us into.

3. ALL ROADS LEAD TO THE BRIDEGROOM

Even if you don't understand bridal lingo, it all goes back to loving the Lord your God with everything you have. This message of the bridegroom is deeply scriptural. I believe the entire word of God is about this culmination of the bride and the bridegroom.

In the bible, we first see John the Baptist referring to Jesus as the bridegroom (John 3:29). Likewise, John the Baptist came in the spirit and power of Elijah to prepare the way of the Lord. John the Baptist's message was one of purity as he prepared a path for Jesus. These truths connect because in the bridal realm, there is a high level of consecration and purity that is needed. The message of purity is how the way is paved for His coming. Just as a bride makes herself ready for her groom, we the church are to do the same in anticipation of the Lord.

In other words, Jesus will return again to capture his bride by his grace with intimacy tied in. This is how Jesus prepared the way for his first coming. This is also how he will prepare the way for his second coming. The message of purity will mark the bridal company of this generation; purity and intimacy with the bridegroom. *The message of preparing the way for the Lord is always through purity.*

Abraham also received the bridal call of intimacy. In fact, his entire life is a picture of this. Abraham's entire journey began as the father of our faith, with the making of a Bride for Jesus in mind. Moses, likewise, led the children of Israel out of Egypt, all for a master plan. This master plan was that a people would be *married* to the bridegroom of God. We see this as God made a covenant of intimacy with the children of Israel in the wilderness. Throughout the scriptures we see a divine thread of God's desire of one day retracting a bride out of the earth to be with Him in his eternal ebode.

The Bridal Family Photo

To illustrate, think of the trinity of God in terms of a family photo. The Lord created man in his image to be with Him in union and bridal intimacy. God created humanity with a great yearning of one day adding a bride, you & me, to the family photo of the already perfected circle of divinity of God the Father, the Son, and the Holy Spirit. We were all created to be with Him in eternal marriage and union as He is with the trinity in love. We are a part of the family photo of divine love and bridal union. God created humanity with a deep desire of adding a bride to the family photo of the Godhead. The Father, Son, and Spirit are all one—in love. They created us to add us to their family photo. They are all three perfected in love. The entire reason we are raising up disciples is to draw them into the bridal realm of intimacy with Jesus Christ. Because he first loved us, we love in return.

Solomon also had a revelation of this truth. Solomon was the wisest man to ever live. Summed up by the end of his life, he gave us the entire purpose of life in Ecclesiastes. All of his wisdom and all that he knew pointed to one instruction, "Love, worship, and know God." Although there was less of an intimate element back then, the consummation of all things leads to two becoming one. The fulfillment of marital union between Jesus and the perfected bride was ever in the heart and mind of the Father.

The Bridegroom Throughout Scripture

The bible is an eternal love letter to the bride. There are 66 books; 1,189 chapters, 31,101 verses, and 783,137 words in the bible. Yet, on the last chapter of the last page in Revelation 22:17, it says, "The Spirit and the Bride say come." This is a foundational verse of my ministry. This overriding theme of a thread of love started from before time and concluded right there in Revelation.

The flood with Noah's Ark points to this theme of eternal intimacy. The kinship and lineage of David, the Holy Spirit on the day of Pentecost, the blinding light of the Apostle Paul were all for the purpose of the end—

which is the eternal beginning. So that one day, we would love, worship, and know God—becoming one with Jesus in martial union and sitting on His throne; just as He sat on his father's throne. God created mankind in his image to one day produce a Bride that would walk with Him intimately. The concluding theme of all of scripture is to be one with the Lord. This is the highest call one could ever obtain. This is the greatest feat, the highest prize, the most valuable achievement that has ever been made available this side of heaven leading into eternity forevermore.

4. THE KNOCKING OF THE BRIDEGROOM

I feel that the Lord's assessment of the church is not the best as of now. Recently, I saw a vision of a major church and there was a big fireweed in the middle of it. I heard the Lord say, "My glory's not there." I feel like if we aren't careful, we could start building on the momentum of "being alive" but, like the Lord says—we're actually dead. Sometimes you can have a reputation of being alive but in Christ's eyes, you are dead. This was the case in the book of revelation with the Sardis church. They had a reputation of being alive yet they were dead in the eyes of the Lord (Revelation 3:1-6). The Lord is calling us higher. In both Sardis and Laodicea, the Lord emphasized pure white garments. He told them to clothe themselves in purity. Ephesians 5:27 says that He is coming back for a bride without spot or blemish: *this is purity*. I believe this to be what the Lord is saying to his bride today. He is calling us to a greater level of loving purity.

My son had a vision coming off of a fast where he saw

Jesus as the judge. The bible says that Jesus is the lamb but that He is also the judge. We see an example of Jesus as the judge in the book of revelation. This is not a time to straddle the fence and have one foot in and one foot out. This is a season for his bridal company; a season in which we need to stay deep in the presence of God. The Lord's standards are not what we think they are. As I mentioned, the Lord's corporate assessment of the church is not very good right now. I am not a doom and gloom guy at all, but I am a *truth* guy. I believe Jesus the bridegroom is wooing us to come into a deeper level of intimacy with Him. I feel that 2020 triggered something leading into this Last Day company of the Bride.

He Stands at the Door and Knocks

To hit home at this point, I recently had a dream on Christmas day at 3:24 A.M. I experienced this dream in both the natural and spiritual. Jesus knocked above my bed. I could hear the knock in the natural. I saw it in my vision and heard it. It was the hand of the Lord knocking very feverently. I felt that the knocking of the Lord, which is found in Revelation 3:20, is a prophetic message to the last day church. It is a last day intimate call to his bride. The Lord desires his bride and is calling her deeper in this season. I believe the Lord is knocking very passionately at the door of His church.

What deeply impacted me about this encounter was the abruptness of the knock that woke me up. Jesus is getting more serious in a passionate, loving way about waking up His bride. I sense that we are in a window of grace where the Lord is knocking to get the attention of His church. The knocking of the Lord goes back to the Church of Laodicea in revelation. Jesus said, "I stand at the door and knock." The Lord is knocking on the doors of our hearts and we need to answer. He is calling us deeper in bridal union. It is a last day prophetic call to the Bride where Jesus offers an invitation to sit at the throne with Him.

Later on, the Lord gave me greater revelation into the dream I had on Christmas. Christmas represents the Lord's coming (His first coming) but the vision of the knocking represents His second coming. Jesus is waking up the church. 3:20 was the scripture but the Lord also revealed revelation to me concerning the extra 4 in 3:24. I feel that this represents the four year grace God has given us.

You'll see corporately in the next four years, the grace of God wooing and calling us. When this four year window shuts it will be harder for it to open. If you're not careful, during this period, you'll miss the opportunity that the Lord desires to come and break bread with you. During this current time of reassessing, we should reassess our priorities. A friend of mine who I deeply honor was sensing the Lord saying something similar. He said to me that he feels purging and purifying is coming to the bride.

It's the Season of the Lord's Return

This purifying will happen before the return of the Lord. We are getting into the last window of Jesus preparing the church for His coming. We are not as far out from the Lord's return as we think we are. I am sure that my children will see the return of the Lord, if not me. I am not setting dates, but I think it is interesting that Bob Jones, a powerful seer and prophetic voice, saw a vision of the future in ten year increments but only saw up to 2060.

Similarly, John Paul Jackson, another major prophetic voice, was born in the 11th month as a sign and a wonder to a generation. When he was born the Lord said he was an 11th hour prophet. He passed away and I believe it is prophetic to where we are on the Lord's timetable. We might not know the day or hour of the Lord's return but we *will* know the season. I believe we are in that season, and are closer than most people think.

5. FOUNDATIONS OF THE BRIDAL COMPANY

"On the third day there was a wedding in Cana of Galilee, and the mother of Jesus was there; and both Jesus and His disciples were invited to the wedding. When the wine ran out, the mother of Jesus said to Him, 'They have no wine.' And Jesus said to her, 'Woman, what does that have to do with us? My hour has not yet come.'

His mother said to the servants, 'Whatever He says to you, do it.' Now there were six stone waterpots set there for the Jewish custom of purification, containing twenty or thirty gallons each. Jesus said to them, 'Fill the waterpots with water.'

So they filled them up to the brim. And He said to them, 'Draw some out now and take it to the head waiter.' So they took it to him. When the headwaiter tasted the water which had become wine, and did not know where it came from (but the servants who had drawn the water knew), the head waiter called the bridegroom, and said to him, 'Every man serves the good wine first, and when the people have drunk freely, then He serves the poorer wine; but you have kept the good wine until now.'

This beginning of His signs Jesus did in Cana of Galilee, and manifested His glory, and His disciples believed in Him." (John 2:1-11 NASB)

Jesus in the flesh is *God with us.* Jesus's first wonder in the bible was to reveal His glory. The first time Jesus reveals His glory is in the bridal paradigm context was at the wedding in which He turned water to wine. This happened during a celebration of two becoming one. You can't blink past this wonder. The deep meaning of this wonder at the wedding is revealed in John 2. At that wedding, Jesus could have waited before revealing His Glory. His hour had not yet come.

Most other times this is mentioned in the context of death on the cross. Mary, his mother, represents love, compassion and hospitality. She tells the servants to do what Jesus asked. She knew Jesus would move on her behalf. You must pay attention to some significant details in this scripture as Jesus is revealing his Glory.

The vessel that Jesus tells the servants to fill represents purification. Jesus tells the servants to fill the vessels up with water; after which He proceeded to turn it into wine. It is prophetic because the Bridegroom always supplies the wine. The fact that Jesus did this wonder at a wedding is a picture of bridal union. Two became one.

The Bridal Realm Reveals God's Glory

John was the only one that penned this story as this account is only in the book of John. The deeper prophetic meaning of this story begins with the 6 vessels. The number 6 represents man. I believe they filled each of those vessels with 20 gallons of water. 6 times 20 equals 120. 120 represents the outpouring of the Spirit upon the upper room. It also demonstrates the purification of the bride and the age of man, the water of the Word and the water baptism of John The Baptist. The Holy Spirit is the seal. He could have chosen anywhere to reveal His glory. For example, He could have revealed His glory at a funeral, because we know He loved to raise the dead; yet it was at a wedding union. The Lord would go on to do many things to reveal His glory like cast out devils. He would go on to demonstrate the forgiveness of sin to display His heart.

He reveals his glory and heart through supernatural access to wealth and provision through the wonder with the coin in the fish's mouth. Throughout the entire span of history where Jesus had one shot to reveal His glory as a sign that He was here, Jesus pops open his treasure map and highlights in capital letters, "THIS IS WHY I AM HERE'—*at the wedding*. "The preparing, capturing, and purifying of My bride, this is why I am here." His journey leads to the glorious end which is the Spirit and the Bride saying "Come." The end is really the beginning; the consummation of the marriage.

Bridal Example of Leadership

It's important as leaders that we steer clear of control and just lead by example and let the chips fall where they may. In order for people to defend the ability to drink they will bring up passages about Jesus drinking wine. For me personally, and I am not trying to debate this, but for me personally—I don't drink. I, in my personal journey, have seen more cons with it than pros.

The Bible says to avoid the appearance of evil. In Matthew 26:29 Jesus said, "Mark my words, I will not drink wine again until I drink wine with you in my Father's kingdom in bridal union." That's why on the cross he spit out the sour wine. There's a nazarite company that the Lord is raising up that is called to a higher standard.

The passages in Luke 14 all point to the wedding, the bridegroom, and the bridal realm. In it, Jesus gives a parable of a wedding feast. He describes the kingdom of heaven and talks about the parable of the ten virgins that took their lamps to meet the bridegroom. Five wise and five foolish virgins point to the message of the bridegroom. It is my favorite parable on this subject. In the Song of Solomon, the entire book is dedicated to the bridal theme, written by the wisest man in history.

A religious spirit blinds people from being able to see the truth of this message. This truth is shown throughout scripture. John the Baptist was in the spirit and power of Elijah and said he must decrease that Jesus might increase. John had the same spirit as Elijah and even wore the same garments as him, both in the spirit and in the natural. The spirit of Elijah on John the Baptist was meant to prepare the Last Day Bride. The spirit of John the Baptist that now rests on this generation is to prepare the bride in purity for Jesus' return. Jesus says Elijah will return again in the end time as one of the two witnesses. This spirit of Elijah will also rest on the bride in the last days.

Two Becoming One

"Husbands, love your wives, just as Christ also loved the church and gave Himself up for her, so that He might sanctify her, having cleansed her by the washing of water with the word, that He might present to Himself the church [a]in all her glory, having no spot or wrinkle or any such thing; but that she would be holy and blameless. So husbands ought also to love their own wives as their own bodies. He who loves his own wife loves himself; for no one ever hated his own flesh, but nourishes and cherishes it, just as Christ also does the church, because we are members of His body. For this reason a man shall leave his father and mother and shall be joined to his wife, and the two shall become one flesh." (Ephesians 5:25-31 NASB)

Paul, the most revelatory man in scripture penned most of the new testament. Paul was never married but wrote more on marriage than anyone. He so walked with the Lord that he, being unmarried, was able to give protocol on it. Paul talks about how the mystery of the marriage is a greater mystery of Christ and the church. Earthly marriage is the lesser reality in comparison to Christ and his church. One day we will not be married. Marital union to Christ is the greater mystery.

Paul goes on to discuss sexual immorality in 1 Corinthian 6:12-19. First he talks about Ephesians 5 in the context of Christian marriage and a righteous unity—the mystery of two becoming one flesh. He then prays that we would become one spirit with the Lord. Both Ephsians 5 and 1 Corthians 6 are gold bars he drops in the context of bridal and marital union. It's a description of our souls becoming married to the Lord like the mystics of old. They reached this place of union and oneness. We have access to this union. Pray that the Lord would help you yield; that you would melt into the eternal reality of who He is.

PART II

BRIDAL GRACE, WORKS, & REWARDS

6. THE BRIDAL COMPANY DISTINCTION

This chapter might be a bit controversial to some—even though I believe the content is clearly laid out throughout scripture. I believe the Lord is calling the bride higher. I want to continue to lay a deep foundation in scripture on this subject. I will just present the revelation, and you can meditate on it and make a decision for yourself. My goal is to focus on the core message of this book; which is the bridal company. Who is the bridal company? The bridal company is *you and me*.

I have traveled and have seen the deepness of those who have been called to be a part of this great company. The bridal company is a people that love Jesus deeply; ones whom Jesus is pulling out of "church as usual." The bridal company goes beyond mere salvation and getting into heaven one day. I believe that the spirit of God is calling his church much higher; to be one with Him.

Drink from different wells

I encourage you to drink from many different wells of the spirit as far as teaching goes. For me, I am hungry and love listening to teaching from people who just love Jesus. I was listening to a Mike Bickle teaching recently. I love Mike Bickle. Mike Bickle talks about having an encounter that wrecked him for life while he was in his twenties. He says he still thinks about it all the time, almost monthly. In the encounter, he went into a dream and Jesus came to Him and said, "You made it in but you wasted the rest of your life."

Mike Bickle woke up out of this encounter weeping on the side of his bed. You have one appointment to look forward to and this appointment is the greatest. It is yet to come—it is when you die and meet the Lord. Out of this encounter, the Lord allowed Mike Bickle to experience the pain of regret from not living his life wholeheartedly. The Lord made it clear that he was saved. He made it in but he wasted his entire christian life. He, referring to Mike Bickle, has been driven by this encounter in a loving way.

Don't waste your Christian life

I once saw a picture before me after coming off a cruise. This vision represented the difference of us becoming His bride versus just being saved and entering into heaven. I saw two cards that we usually have on our Glory Cruises. The regular card gives you access to your room. Then you have the gold card. The gold card is used to get into a special room we rent for speakers as a green room. Both cards get you in and you still have the full experience of the boat. The boat represents heaven where there is no more pain, tears, or sorrows.

The gold card from the vision represents greater intimacy and closeness to Jesus. It gives you greater reward, access and treatment. Our assistant gets treated like a king when we put this room under his name. He jokingly says, "I'll take it if I have to." This is how it is with the Lord and our journey to heaven. My prayer is that we would all go for it and that we would all have the gold card in heaven as the bride of Christ. It's important that you understand both cards get you on the ship. Yet one of them provides you with a place of greater access and intimacy.

I believe there is a company that God is giving 'Gold cards' to; greater access to intimacy. Something deep within me just drives me to live a life fully surrendered to Him. You see clearly in scripture that our surrender here on earth counts to the Lord.

I am reminded of a famous statement by Leonard Ravenhill which says, "This life is a dressing room for eternity." Yieldedness and your works determine how you are dressed for eternity. How you spend this life should be based on your intended heavenly blueprint. Intent is important here. The Lord knew you before you were in your mother's womb. He has a blueprint for your life. All you have to do is obey what He told you.

Don't forget that as you step further into your call, it's

as simple as doing what he told you to do. Don't worry about the crowds or what people want or think. Just obey and do what he tells you to do. This is ministry—to do what the Lord says. That's the entire Christian walk.. We have one life to yield and recalibrate to the heavenly blueprint set up for us—which will reflect in our eternal posture forever. There are no participation rewards in heaven, where everyone gets the same trophy. Things are the very opposite in heaven's protocol.

I believe we need to be reminded of this from a scriptural standpoint. Especially in today's society and where culture is going. In our current culture everyone gets a reward, everyone is treated equally. They are trying to neutralize everything, and this is not how God set things up.This is not his true relational nature. I say all of this because I believe we need a healthy 'wooing' of the Spirit unto Him. In this, we will find ourselves distinct and separated as the true bridal company.

7. EMPOWERED BY GRACE

I want to give you a scriptural premise for what has been discussed. I would love it if everyone just got saved and received the same reward. I would subscribe to that theology anyday, but this is not the way it is. This thinking is not biblical and to be clear I am not trying to make salvation harder for anyone. I just love the truth. He is the way and the truth. "You shall know the truth," Jesus said, "and it shall set you free" (see John 8). In 2 Corinthians 5:10, the scripture makes it clear that "we must all appear before the judgment seat of Christ, that each one may receive the things *done* in the body, according to what he has done, whether good or bad." Did you read that? What is *done* in the body; whether good or bad.

According to 1 Corinthians 3:8, each one will receive his own reward according to his own labor. Both these verses emphasize rewards, works, and what we have done. Revelation 22:12 states, "I am coming soon, bringing my reward with me to repay all people according to their deeds."

Revelation 2:23 declares, "I am He who searches the minds and hearts. And I will give to each one of you according to your works."

I know some would say, "Well what about the fact that I am saved by grace?" You have to be careful in current culture. There is a heavy grace talk, which I love. I even appreciate the term *hyper-grace*, because I believe God's grace can't be over exaggerated. You can't make the real grace of God more *hyper* than it already is. God's grace is completely supernatural. It's His empowerment to live holy.

Let me explain it this way: Salvation is free. This can get very blurred because people say things like, "I live by grace." This is true, you're saved by grace but good works are heavily threaded throughout scripture. I suggest that you reread the bible if you believe that it isn't. Those who know me know that I am not Martha or Ishmael at all. I am one of the biggest condoners of Mary over Martha and teach it often. However, Jesus said if you love me you will obey my commands. This is *works* through intimacy. The true Mary's actually work a lot. You clearly see the reward and works. If you're wondering where intimacy is in all of this—they're inseparable and that's where I am building to.

True works rewarded by Jesus are saturated, bathed, and birthed out of intimacy. I quote Matthew 7:22 all the time. Jesus said that many, many will come to Him on that day and say, "Lord, Lord did I not cast out devils in your name, prophesy in your name, and do many mighty exploits in your name?" But Jesus says to them, "Depart from me you workers of iniquity, I never knew you." Why did this happen? Because these were works not done out of intimacy. If you truly love the Lord you will work and obey Him. Jesus even says, "My food is to do the will of My Father." Our food is to *do* His will and there is ease and a grace in it. I really want to clear the air on these things because of the current grace talks. Grace is good, but if not understood can blur our need to *do* and work for the Lord.

In Revelation 2, Jesus rebukes the church of Ephesus, telling them to return to their first love. He tells them to repent and to *do* their first works over again. Jesus tells the church of Ephesus to get back to their first love and intimacy. You just can't separate the two. Works done out of intimacy are throughout scripture. Keep in mind, the verses I just mentioned are from the New Testament and from the mouth of Jesus directly. I want to empower you through this to love Him *better*. Psalm 62:12 talks about his loving kindness and being rewarded according to His works. Through these principles I want to build us into the bridal company.

If we are not careful, sometimes I see that many are just trying to get by in this thing. This is not good and the enemy desires this. He wants to just put a blanket of getting by on people and just calm them down. He says, "Don't be so full of the Holy Spirit, don't be so zealous and just tone it down." If he can't get you to backslide and cause you to end up in hell—he will cause you to stand before the Lord in regret, like Mike Bickle experienced in his vision. You don't want Jesus to say, "You are saved but you wasted your entire Christian life." This is not meant to be a heavy thing but to instill in you a desire to be set on fire for Jesus. In that place, we no longer worry about the cares of this life but desire to be set ablaze for Jesus.

8. YIELDING TO THE BRIDEGROOM

Obeying Jesus takes precedence

I have learned that the more busy I get, the more efficient I have to be with my time. I say this because of how hectic my schedule is. I personally don't have a lot of time for myself anymore; which is fine. I don't want it, don't need it. I have learned that intimacy with Jesus is first and foremost.

Jesus, stated, "If you love me you will obey my commandments." The Ministry in its purest form is simply doing what He told you to do. This is in addition to loving Jesus and family extremely well. True ministry in its purest form is obeying Jesus out of intimacy. Jesus is the unadulterated model for ministry and he only did what he saw the Father doing and said what the Father was saying. Obeying Jesus takes precedence over family for it to run the way it was meant to in love, unity and the blessing of God. Jesus said that anyone that looks back after putting hands to the plow is not worthy of Him. He literally stated, "Anyone that loves mother or father more than me is not worthy of me." That's hard for some to swallow but it's very biblical. Love Jesus, obey Jesus then family after that.

> "Whoever then breaks one of the least of these commandments, and teaches others to do the same, shall be called least in the kingdom of heaven; but whoever keeps and teaches them, he shall be called great in the kingdom of heaven." (Matthew 5:19)

In this verse you see the levels of achievement. Jesus is crystal clear on this and makes no bones about it. Jesus says if you don't obey the least of these teachings you will be least in the kingdom of heaven. It's very much works-based but it is works-based *out of intimacy.* I try to be one of the greatest promoters of the message of intimacy with Jesus. But if we are not careful we can become unbalanced and negate the value of good works and it gets a bad wrap. In reality, the purest form of works that exist are all birthed out of intimacy.

Romans 2:6 says "He," referring to Jesus, "will repay each person according to their works." I love this theme in scripture. I feel the wind of God on this topic. We are kidding ourselves if we don't think that there is a cost to these things. Jesus becoming everything in our lives is more than just talk. It means we are completely given over to Jesus in surrender. Our desire should be that our entire lives count when we meet Him someday and that we are closest in proximity which is in union with Him. The scripture says, "He who is joined to the Lord is one spirit with Him" (1 Corinthians 6:17). I myself don't want to be least but greatest in closeness and proximity. We must desire to be just like Him, in holy infatuation. As I said previously, it all started and will end with the Spirit and the Bride saying, "Come."

Bridal obedience

You can hammer the secret place and intimacy all you want but if there is no yieldedness or obedience to the Lord—you're off. I was talking to my kids about this subject recently concerning ministering and ministry. I have these conversations with them now because they are getting older and they have questions. I can tell that the Lord has been speaking to them. They're coming into their calling. So I have been teaching them on more mature levels. I was telling them about me personally and how I approach things. If I am a mouth piece and an ambassador for the Lord and I have my choice, I will usually preach intimacy and falling madly in love with Jesus. But to be clear now the voice of God always trumps this. I don't always get to preach what I want to preach.

    I was explaining to my kids that you have to be careful. If the Lord spoke to you specifically to preach or teach in a certain direction and you veer somewhere else, you are outside of obedience. You might even think that your preferred sermon is urgent and top priority—yet if God hasn't inspired it, it's disobedience. This can cause you to miss the Lord and this is not true intimacy. In this, you are basically teaching the thing that you yourself are not walking out. Ministry in its purest form is obeying the Lord. You really just want to hammer into obeying Him and loving Him.

> "For no other foundation can anyone lay than that which is laid, which is Jesus Christ. Now if anyone builds on this foundation with gold, silver, precious stones, wood, hay, straw, each one's work will become clear; for the Day will declare it, because it will be revealed by fire; and the fire will test each one's work, of what sort it is. If anyone's work which he has built on it endures, he will receive a reward. If anyone's work is burned, he will suffer loss; but he himself will be saved, yet so as through fire." (1 Corinthians 3:11-15)

In this again we see works highlighted. You might be wondering, *I thought this book was about bridal intimacy.* It is—but you cannot separate the works of the Lord from intimacy. If we are not careful we can get so caught up in lingo in our generation that we can miss Him. You can get *religious* in the vain of intimacy. I want us to get to a place of surrender where we are so in love with Him and pliable in His hands. That's what belief in the Lord entails; your life becomes so yielded and dependent upon Him. Our posture should declare, "Whatever I am doing, Lord, I just want to obey You." If we are not careful we can take even a revelation from the Lord—a true revelation that is upright and directly from the lord and we grab hold of it so tight that we quench the flow of the Spirit. You can even do this with intimacy especially when we separate it from obedience.

9. HEAVENLY REWARDS

In Revelation 19:5, from the throne, came a voice saying, "Praise our God, all you his servants, you who fear Him, from the least to the greatest." There it goes again; you see a clear *difference* in heaven. There are not matching trophies; it's clear from scripture. This verse deals with all of His church and body. This passage mentions all that are saved, from the least to the greatest. This is not meant to be heavy but we have one life to get this right. Yesterday is already gone, we can't get it back. The famous scripture says, "Lord give me this day my daily bread." There is manna from heaven for us right now. Let us not miss His daily bread so we can go to a deeper dimension in Him. We can go deeper into Him and become more like Him as we receive His daily bread. As we do this we will stack up a greater reward on the other side where we will reign.

In the previous chapter we read 1 Corinthians 3:11-15. In it, we see that anyone that builds with gold, silver, or precious stone their works make it through the fire. In actuality their works become more purified as they go through it. Gold, silver and precious stone would be the true works of deep intimacy with the Lord. If you have the foundation as Jesus Christ and you are trying to build upon that, your works are stone.

This was a message to the *church* in Corinth that had nothing to do with the Lost. It was to Christians directly. Earlier I referenced the passage which says many will come saying, "Lord, Lord, I prophesied in your name." "Prophesied in your name," represents *wood*. "I cast out devils in your name," represents *hay* and "did mighty exploits in your name," is *straw*. The fire on that day burned up all these works of wood, hay, and straw. Through intimacy we yield and obey and that produces gold. Silver represents the voice of the Lord which will only be purified by fire and become more valuable. Only yielding to the voice of the Lord through intimacy will stand the test of fire. We can be saved but the reward will not be there, based on scripture. The reward is based on how we lived out our lives here on the earth. Not only that but you also see you can lose your reward. Revelation 3:11 says:

> "I am coming soon. Hold fast what you have, so that no one may seize your crown."

Revelation Rewards

In Revelation chapter 2 and 3 there is a correction and an encouragement given in each word from Jesus...but you also see a reward at the end. I call them *Revelation rewards*. These rewards are made available to the churches throughout the entire church age. The last and greatest reward is given in the context of proximity and becoming one with the Lord in union. This is clearly based on scripture the highest prize made available. Concerning the church of Ephesus, you have the reward being the right to eat at the tree of life in the paradise of God. The church of Smyrna is given the crown of life and will not be hurt by the second death.

The church of Pergamum is given the hidden manna and a white stone with a new name on it. The church of Thyatira is given the authority of the nations and a morning star. The church of Sardis is dressed in white and its name will never be blotted out of the book of life. The church of Philadelphia is made a pillar in the temple of God. The last church was Laodicea, which was granted to sit with Jesus on His throne just as He sat with His father on the throne. I read this afresh and thought to myself, *you have got to be kidding me. This reward makes the others look like consolation prizes. The reward of sitting with Jesus upon his throne!*

I am not trying to be sacrilegious or anything, but instead attempting to make a point. I want all of these rewards deeply but *this* is what I am after: to sit with Jesus upon the throne. The answer to the last days' church age is this bridal union of deep intimacy, in which Jesus stands at the door and knocks.

As we open the door he promises to come in and dine with us. This represents intimate union. What triggers the reward of sitting on his throne is deep intimacy. This is why I am calling the bride to focus deeply on this last reward. This manifestation has been showing up in very real ways, as I told you about in a previous chapter concerning my encounter on Christmas. It's the last church age, it's the window we stepped into where he is really going after his bride. The climax of what God is after in all of this is the heart of his bride. Jesus is at the door knocking.

There's no excuse for neglecting prayer

If you look at Luke chapter 4, you'll see a progression of parables that the Lord goes after. The Lord goes into a wedding feast parable, and right after he goes into a great banquet parable. He emphasized a wedding feast and then a more broad banquet. The word says in the book of Psalms that the Lord's promises are purified seven times over which means that there are layers to what He is doing.

There was an encounter in which a powerful prophet I highly respect tells a story of a girl that was praying for her father. He was bitter and isolated Himself from everyone but got saved at the last minute. This prophet went up to heaven and saw this old man. The old man made it into Heaven but he lived on the outskirts of heaven and had a greatly diminished reward and a lack of proximity to the Lord.

Another encounter that emphasizes this is a story about a Korean pastor of a Megachurch. He owned about a 150 million dollar church property. He had a stroke and went to heaven but was blown away because there were several things that the Lord asked Him. The Lord rebuked this pastor hard in love about his time in the word and in prayer. Because he had gotten busy in ministry, he had cut back on prayer, this pastor saw different degrees of reward. He told the pastor, "Busyness is no excuse for neglecting time in prayer."

10. PARABLE OF THE BRIDESMAIDS

I want to open this chapter by looking at my favorite parable given by Jesus. It is found in Matthew 25, and details the story of 10 bridesmaids. I love it because the content that comes out of it is of intimacy with the Lord. Intimacy entails shutting the door and being with Him. In the parable, there are ten virgins; five are wise and five are foolish. We see that the only thing that separated them was the oil or the lack thereof. In that parable they are all dressed as bridesmaids and all carried lamps. They were all going in the same direction. I believe this parable clearly speaks to the body of Christ. It's important to the season we are in, that those with extra time on their hands should maximize it. It's about *oil, oil, oil!*

This is a time that we want to reset the pattern of our lives to become an *oily* people. We are to be people that have lamps overflowing with oil. Then, when things return to normal, we learn to sustain the oil from this season.

That's why I am going to show you the difference with these bridesmaids and what the oil represented versus the preachers in Matthew 7. The bridesmaids fell asleep and became drowsy from the journey and Jesus did not rebuke any of them over this. Then midnight came, representing a new day, and there was a doorway there where you could enter into the wedding with the bridegroom. The highest goal in life is to be with the bridegroom. But because there was not enough oil, the five foolish couldn't get through the door.

Significance of the oil

The oil is what is produced in the secret place. It's the crushing of the olives which produces the Kabod glory; the weighty glory of God and intimacy. Continuously being with Him produces more of the spirit and oil in our lives.The oil is costly. That's why the wise would not give it up and why the foolish had to go buy more oil. The five foolish went to buy more oil and came back but the door had been shut. They cried out to Him, "Lord, Lord" and Jesus said back to them, "I do not know you." This speaks of a current intimate relationship with Jesus Christ. That word, 'know' is the same word in the greek that Joseph used when talking about not knowing Mary when she got pregnant with Jesus.

Jesus is saying I never at any point knew you. If we are not careful we can learn the rhythm of faith and the word.

We believe the word but the bible even says that demons believe Jesus is the son of God but hell awaits them. You can yield your life in a natural manner to trigger spiritual implications of prophesying, casting out devils, and mighty exploits but if they were not done out of intimately knowing Jesus then it becomes works of iniquity; which means you can set on a course of learning the ways of ministry. You learn how to tap into the ways of the Spirit but have earthly motives. This can put you in a vein in which you never know Jesus intimately yet are still doing ministry.

Ten bridesmaids had oil at one time. Yet only some of them had it when it counted the most. That's why it's so important to you and I that we become hoarders of oil which is the most valuable thing in life. If you had to ask me from here to the return of the Lord what is the most important thing you should do, I would say hoarding and sustaining your oil. Which is intimately *being with Him*. Not having enough oil caused them to miss the arrival of the bridegroom. He didn't say to them, "I never knew you." He says, "I currently do not know you." They are all virgins which means that there is a purity there, they are all going to find the bridegroom.

It's important that we cut out the entanglements of life to focus on Jesus. I am sure we all know people that had oil at one time; they were burning bright for Jesus but they came away from this focus and the oil diminished. *The bridal company is about always increasing in oil and sustaining oil.* I don't know anything more valuable than this. I want to point this out because the bridal company looks different than the rest. You can't ride off last year's oil. You can not live off of yesterday's manna. It's an *ongoing* relationship.

PART III

A BRIDE MADE READY

11. CLOSENESS WITH THE BRIDEGROOM

Some may wonder why Jesus says in Revelation, "He that has ears, let him hear what the Spirit says to the churches." There are some things God left kind of general in scripture to see how far people would try to go in Him. He wanted to see if we would simply read it at a surface level or dig deeper. In this, he would see the seeking on our part, which is out of a pure love and desire for Him. In the middle of John's vision in Revelation, Jesus pauses to utter, "Blessed are they."

In that encounter you hear a broad voice from the throne that said, "Worship God all who fear Him from the least to the greatest." Then it goes on to say, "The bride has prepared herself and has made herself ready. She is clothed in white linen which is the righteous deeds of the saints." The angels write all of this down and they say, "Blessed are those that are invited to the wedding feast of the lamb" (Revelation 19:9).

Some would say, "Well this is for everyone that is

saved." Yet we see distinctions from the least to the greatest. I want to be found in this *greatest* company and I want to have oil. I never want to hear the Lord say, "I don't know you" or to say, "You were burning years ago but you let the cares of this life and the fear of man talk louder than My wooing voice of intimacy." May the main stamp on us, as the bridal company, be intimacy with Him and following His voice of driving love. Everything else is amazing and included, but *intimacy* should be the driving force.

In the bible, Jesus gives a parable about the seed and the soil of the heart. We all know that there is a company that has different soil that the word, or seed, falls upon. Some fall on fertile soil, producing sixty and up to one hundred fold returns. Some fall upon the path and plant roots while others fall on rocks and the roots don't go deep. For those that are born again, it is intimacy that keeps your soil pure and soft.

As the seeds fall, they continually grow in destiny and then they will sprout and produce one hundred fold. But those that keep the soil cluttered with rocks and the cares of this world will not yield the righteous acts of others that become your clothing in the bridal realm. We are at our best when we're in God, no matter what we are called to. Even in business, you will run that better clothed in intimacy with God. But we see here deeds are on our end and they have to do with yieldness and a production out of closeness with the Lord. The purest driving force behind all of this is intimacy with the Lord.

The Bridegroom rebukes in love

With the church of Laodicea, Jesus says, "Buy from me." It's important that we note he says this to the church. He loved the church but rebuked them in love. Every church was given encouragement, rebuke, remedy and reward. He tells the church to buy from Him white garments that they may not be ashamed of their nakedness. The white garments that we see are the righteous deeds of the saints. Jesus used the term *buy from me* to relay this.

Remember the oil from the bridesmaids? They had to go and buy because the oil was costly. It's a costly life—yielded and laid down to intimate love. Make no mistake, salvation is free and we can not, under any circumstances, buy salvation. When Jesus uses the term 'buy' he perfectly understands that the blood of Jesus is free, as well as salvation.

> "...for all have sinned and fall short of the glory of God, being justified freely by his grace through the redemption that is in Christ Jesus..." (Romans 3:23-24)

Yet, regarding other aspects of our faith, whenever you start hearing the lingo of 'buying' in scripture it refers to something being costly on our end. This is where it steps outside of salvation alone and brings a need on our part for obedience and yieldedness. This is why the other five foolish bridesmaids had to go buy more oil. You can enter into heaven and be unclothed fully according to the righteous deeds and yieldedness to Him through love. So we must understand that there is a preparation of ourselves from an abandoned love and radical obedience; which is separated from salvation alone.

If you are one of those that think it's enough to just be saved, I say this: if you would just take a month of time with Jesus I believe he would set your heart burning bright to know Him. We are called to this deep burning infatuation with Him. If we are not careful, the cares of this life and the devil can start to blur that realm. The devil is the prince of the powers of the air and blinds the minds of the unbelievers. He wants to make us okay with just getting in and going to heaven. However, with the bridal company, there is just a different tone to their voice and a different level of intimacy with the Lord.

12. INGREDIENTS OF THE BRIDAL COMPANY: PURITY

There are three main aspects or attributes of the bride I want to focus on in this section. These three attributes will always be a part of the makeup of the bridal company. I see these three umbrellas as being the key to everything concerning the bride flowing as it should. These three are again inseparable from the bride. The first attribute is *purity*. Many people hear me hit on this a lot in our ministry. I do so because it is paramount in the makeup of the bride. You see it throughout scripture. Purity is always linked to the bride. So when I begin to talk about the bridal company, it's to inspire to yield and inspire to walk in purity on this side of heaven. We will continue to see a greater increase in purity among God's people as he prepares his bride. That's why the spirit of Elijah always foreruns the Lord.

For example, we see this through John the Baptist at Jesus's first coming. John prepared the way of the Lord and his main message was repentance and purity paving the way of the crooked paths into the highway of holiness. The highway of holiness is for Jesus to come. During the end times, the Spirit of Elijah is going to come again as one of the two witnesses (Revelation 11). These two will prophesy for three and a half years and pave the way for the Lord's final coming. They will be persecuted and the bible says they will die in the streets.

They will have the same powers as Moses and Elijah. One of the two witnesses, the bible says, has the power to shut up the heavens; which is what Elijah did. He decreed a drought and then he opened the heavens again with his prayers. The other had the power to turn waters into blood and call plagues to the earth. We see the same resume with Moses in Egypt. After these two prophets lay in the streets for three and a half days, they will supernaturally be raised from the dead and there will be an earthquake.

Your purity reflects your intimacy

So as we draw closer to the coming of the Lord, you will see an increase and emphasis on purity. My prayers are that we may be as His bride, a people that are continually yielding to purity. When you see purity compromised, the bridal realm will be jeopardized. The level of one's purity reflects the level of intimacy. The same goes for character. Some people may appear to be unstained with this world but they are quick to take offense, quick to gossip, quick to submit to fear, doubt, murmuring. So when I am talking about purity I am talking about character as well.

I say this because some people look untainted since they grew up in church. They don't involve themselves with the things of this world and they look pure. But their hearts are not right. The bible says that the pure in heart shall see God. Some look pure on the outside but are easily offended. The bible speaks against being easily offended. When you are full of the spirit of God, it's hard to be easily offended. Purity comes from intimacy but there is also a deeper yielding on our part. Other common issues are gossip and quick to complain and murmur. The bridal company does not involve herself in gossip or submits herself to fear. The bridal company is so caught up in love with Jesus and what He thinks about them that they couldn't care less.

Purity is a matter of the heart

Paying attention when compromising to yield to the level of purity begins to become easier. Some would read this and say well, I am not in blatant sin. We must understand that purity is down to the depths of the heart. It's without a spot or wrinkle. It's about having clean hands and a pure heart. It's also about correct motives. For instance, there are people who don't involve themselves in a lot of bad things yet their motives are impure. There's selfish ambition there; things driving them that are impure. There is no condemnation for those that struggle because we all have, but may we be a people that are constantly allowing the Spirit to wash over us like a river. Purity involves both the outer and the inner qualities of who we are in reflection to His likeness.

I want to make it clear that purity is required. That's why we see in scripture she, meaning the bride, prepared herself. There is cooperation on our end required. Salvation is free but Jesus said buy from me white garments. There is a cost. Sometimes, if we are not careful, we can focus too heavily on the grace and the salvation of God and neglect other necessities. Cooperation and yieldedness is clear in scripture:

> "...that He might present her to Himself a glorious church, not having spot or wrinkle or any such thing, but that she should be holy and without blemish." (Ephesians 5:27)

The main attribute that Jesus presents in the bride is her being "without spot or wrinkle." She should be without any other blemish. Instead, she will be holy and without fault. It's really interesting to note that Paul writes that this attribute is what Jesus is preparing her for. The purity factor meant the most to Jesus in preparing the bride in Him. We must allow his presence to purify us. Jesus's blood makes us righteous. We know this but there is a yieldness that he requires that we walk out.

> "Let us be glad and rejoice and give Him glory, for the marriage of the Lamb has come, and His wife has made herself ready." (Revelation 19:7-8)

As we read this verse we see that it has nothing to do with sovereignty. Through his grace and love, we are empowered to make ourselves ready. The bible says she made herself ready in connection with the bride. We read that she, meaning the bride, has been given the finest of white garments. You better believe that heaven is the height of all luxury. If you have ever had a heavenly encounter you see this real fast. The finest in pure white linen refers to holiness and purity without blemish. The fine linen represents the good deeds of God's people or the righteous deeds of the saints.

The bride wears purity in heaven; it's all white. It's made up of the righteous deeds done in the flesh—the deeds of God's holy people. I did a study on linen, which is what we will be wearing, and this is what I found. Linen is more expensive and it's not easy to manufacture. Linen was a sign of wealth in ancient times. No fabric can outperform linen in natural strength and durability. It has two to three times the strength of cotton. Fine Linen has no slubs or lumps and is very constant. This is in total agreement with the nature of heaven.

Bridal garments of purity reflect Heaven

So again, the righteous deeds play a part in what it takes to make up in yieldedness. Jesus says to buy from Him white garments; which represents the costly nature of yielding to Jesus. It becomes a lot easier when you are infatuated in love with Jesus to live yielded. Scripture backs this premise and the revelation of fine linen.

We see this in Revelation 15:6. There are seven angels that hold the seven plagues in the last days, all dressed in all fine linen. The bible goes out of its way to highlight what these angels are wearing. This is because there is great significance in it. Their garments represent purity. In Proverbs 31:22, you see the Proverbs 31 woman is dressed in fine linen. You even see the high priests were required to wear fine linen to even enter into the inner courts. My prayer is that our lives would yield these righteous deeds that buy from Jesus the white garments of purity and holiness.

As we continue to look at the importance of purity to the bride, James 1:27 speaks of pure and undefiled religion before God the Father. It gives us a call to visit orphans and widows in their trouble, and to keep oneself unspotted from the world. We see in this verse that the purest form of religion to God before the father is to look after orphans and widows in their distress. You also see this 'keeping herself pure' and a posture of yielding on the behalf of the bride. Likewise, you see in 2 Timothy 2:20-21 which says:

> "In a wealthy home some utensils are made of gold and silver, and some are made of wood and clay. The expensive utensils are used for special occasions, and the cheap ones are for everyday use."

This passage is very interesting. You even see a

different company within this passage that Paul is writing about. The passage says expensive utensils are used for special occasions and cheap ones for everyday use. You can hear this bridal company in this passage. The rest of the passage states.

> If you keep yourself pure, you will be a special utensil for honorable use. Your life will be clean, and you will be ready for the Master to use you for every good work.

Basically, he is saying you want to be the expensive utensils; the bridal company set apart for special use. If you want to be invited into the wedding feast, as the silver and gold, then the main qualification that Paul writes is to keep yourself pure. We must keep ourselves pure and undefiled from the world. We need to pray that Jesus would give us a fresh standard of purity. He is loving and kind and it's His love that leads us to repentance.

To diminish purity is to neglect the bridal realm of the spirit

So He calls us higher and into greater purity. The scriptures say that the fervent prayer of the righteous availeth much (James 5:16). You can pray fervently all you want but if there is no righteousness then it's to no effect. The scriptures say we are to seek first his righteousness and all these other things will be added. Again, righteousness comes first. If you start playing around with purity, you can't just forget about verses that carry heavy blessings and promises to be fulfilled. The bride is pure and this goes back to Ephesians 5.

He desires to present the bride to Himself. He wants to pull the bride out of the corruption of this world and, without spot or wrinkle, present her to Himself. We know this is by His grace and His blood. Nobody can do this on their own. However, there is work on our part as we have seen. Purity is a non-negotiable. You can have the bridal talk but if there is inconsistency in the realm of purity, it doesn't match up on the eternal side and in the spirit. When you start diminishing purity you start negating that bridal realm.

13. INGREDIENTS OF THE BRIDAL COMPANY: INTIMACY

The second ingredient is that the bride will maintain a fiery love for Jesus that supersedes any other. So basically the three ingredients that make up the bride are purity, intimacy, love, and obedience. When any of these are missing these do not equate to a bridal dimension. When these are intact many others just fall into place naturally. Like humility, character and many other things.

So again we have she, meaning the bride will maintain a fiery love that supersedes any other. The oil of the spirit that joins the bride to the Lord is all that matters. That means the oil that we talk about in Matthew 25 in the lamp that gets you through the door into the wedding feast with the bridegroom king stays full. The bride possesses this unquenchable fiery love and maintains it because it means the most to her in everyday life. The oil that enables her, the bride, to be one in spirit with the Lord is of most importance. That oil is of first love and sustained love. I want to land this point with a look at Song of Solomon writing from the point of view of the bride to the bridegroom.

> *"Place me like a seal over your heart,*
> *like a seal on your arm.*
> *For love is as strong as death,*
> *its jealousy is as enduring as the grave.*
> *Love flashes like fire,*
> *the brightest kind of flame.*
> *Many waters cannot quench love,*
> *nor can rivers drown it.*
> *If a man tried to buy love*
> *with all his wealth,*
> *his offer would be utterly scorned."*
> (Song of Solomon 8:6-7)

The word *seal* in hebrew also carries the same meaning as a signet ring; which is really the position that the Holy Spirit plays in the life of a believer. It comes from the root latin word *signum* meaning *sign*. It would usually have the initials of the person in the ring. You would press it into hot wax and seal documents or decrees with it. You see her saying place me like a *seal* on your heart. She goes to the heart first. This is intentional. She also says, *as a seal on your arm*. A seal is an unbreakable bond that the spirit does with us as the bride. Jesus Christ is the signet ring. He is the oil, so to speak, that culminates the union.

Yet you see bridal love in the form of a seal on both the heart and the arm. With the heart being mentioned first and the arm second. This is on purpose because the seal of bridal love and union and oneness with Him is in the progression of the first and second commandments. Loving the Lord your God with all your heart is first. This is intimacy and the bridal realm meaning heart first. Second, the arm signifies loving your neighbor as yourself. The arm speaks of works and strength; which is a picture of loving your neighbor.

You will always see the initial driving force in fulfilling the will of God for the bridal company is love, intimacy and infatuation. The second command to love our neighbor is just as important as the first. One without the other and they both fall apart. Everything is complete in these two commandments. Basically these two commandments sum up the law and the prophets. Continuing to study Song of Solomon 8:6-7 the scripture says:

> *"For love is as strong as death,*
>   *its jealousy as enduring as the grave.*
>   *Love flashes like fire..."*

This is the type of love that I have been talking about and is one of the main attributes of the bride. It's a non negotiable that the bride carries. There are different degrees of love even in the context of loving your neighbor. This realm right here is in the bridal realm of Song of Solomon. It's deeply passionate and the highest form of love.

> "Many waters cannot quench love,
>   nor can rivers drown it.
>   If a man tried to buy love
>   with all his wealth,
>   his offer would be utterly scorned..."

We get this type of love especially where everything is going. She essentially says to the bridegroom in this verse, *look I am memorized, infatuated with you. Place me as a seal on your heart.* Meaning, *brand me into union and oneness with you. Seal me to you in the spirit and on your arm that I may love you with my heart, soul and mind and my neighbor as myself.*

She compares love to the strongest thing known to man and says love is as strong as death. She comes out the gate comparing her love for the bridegroom to be as strong as death. Meaning for us that the strength of bridal love is as strong as death even when faced by it. That word *death* in this context means *plague*. Death is a force you can't avoid—in fact, it is forced upon you.

Yielding even unto persecution

We know that in the times we are in, according to Matthew 24, Jesus said, "You will be persecuted for my name sake." Basically even when faced with death by natural means or through persecution, the love for the bridegroom is as strong as natural or forced death as a result of persecution. Love is the only force stronger than death. This is the main thing it has to drive all of who we are in life. If there is any other driving force than bridal love there are going to be chinks in your armor. But when bridal love is the main source that drives you, even in the face of death or persecution—you would give up everything for love. The only time death loses its power is when love is brought into the equation. Namely, love for Jesus Christ. The bridal company is willing to die for Jesus because of love for Him.

Our school has personally put out martyrs. I had an encounter where I was somewhere in my bed and was awakened into an encounter. I was being crucified and I felt the spikes go through my hand. Around the same time of this encounter the first martyr from our bible college was killed in Yemen. Love is so strong that even when this type of death is presented to you—*love wins*.

Jesus says if you deny me before men I will deny you before my father in heaven. This is personally how I teach my own kids. I advise you to do the same because it's the Bible. I told them, "Gun to your head or knife to your throat—the pain for just a short second. It's not even a question. We choose Jesus." Jesus is everything. The Holy Spirit again is the signet ring. Look at Peter's life pre-Holy Spirit. The bridegroom Jesus was on the earth and walked with them. But Peter, prior to the the signet ring of the Holy Spirit coming into the picture, is faced with death and denies Jesus three times.

This is a great indicator of who the Holy Spirit is and his ministry to us. Peter loved Jesus; He walked hand in hand with the spotless lamb of God. Yet he denied Christ because the Holy Spirit is the strength and is the oil in our lamps that keeps that love burning that is stronger than death. *That's why it's important that you pray in the Holy Spirit constantly and be full of the Holy Ghost.*

Stay full of the Holy Spirit and the word of God. In this, you will be able to say, "Present me with whatever you want. I choose Jesus." Bridal love is the greatest force burning through to humanity. You can not beat a bridal company in love with Jesus. But when there is not strong bridal love there are motives that the enemy can play on. He will sift you like wheat, the bible says. Bridal love purges and keeps us pure. It doesn't fear man and there are no false motives in it.

After the Holy Spirit was sent on the day of Pentecost, Peter was filled and then became the spokesman for the church. He boldly preached the word. When you fast forward and see what happens when he is presented with death, not only does he take it but church history confirms but he asked to be crucified upside down because he didn't feel worthy to be crucified in the manner of the Lord Jesus Christ.

Why? Because death doesn't have a chance against bridal love. You see the strongest people tremble and fall back at the thought of persecution. Yet you see the frailest of people, when faced with persecution, are so infatuated and caught up in bridal love that they are like giants in the spirit, unwavering at the threat of death. The strength of authentic bridal love is unmatched.

> "Many waters cannot quench love,
> nor can rivers drown it."

Notice she mentions the love cannot be quenched or drowned—referring to fire. Burning love is a vertical pull, and it's the greatest thing you can involve yourself with in this life. You will never see a sideways chimney...it always burns up. At first the verse focuses on the vertical ministry then shifts to the horizontal. The waters of this world that are horizontal represent the horizontal ministry. These are the lesser horizontal distractions of life that flow from east to west. If these lesser things can put out your flame with the Lord this is a great gauge that you need more oil. We need our flame burning brighter.

May our love burn so bright that death and sheol are a joke. The cares of this world and the waters that try and put it out are a joke. Why? Because many waters can not quench this love. The bride, in Song of Solomon, begins to work her way down to the lesser enemies of love. That, while yet lesser in strength, are still very real and always attempt to threaten the strength of this love that must be maintained. The second main attribute that marks the bride is that she *maintains*.

She possesses this fiery burning love that is unquenchable. It burns so bright and full that the many waters of this world can't put it out. Even death cannot put it out and has no chance. That's why if we are like Peter and we focus too much on the storms and the cares of this world we can start to sink and not be walking toward union with Jesus. If these voices of this world start to diminish your flame it's not a condemning thing. It's just a healthy point that we need to fall deeper in love with Jesus. As she jumps from death not stopping love, to fire, then water, she narrows the focus down to an *even* lesser distraction:

> *"If a man tried to buy love*
> *with all his wealth,*
> *his offer would be utterly scorned."*

She makes a very valuable point in the arena of wealth. Even Satan tempted Jesus with this one. Money is up there in power. You can see these tiers that the bride jumps through (death, fire, water, distractions, wealth) and says love is more powerful than them all. This point boils down to this: if you can be bought...check your love with Jesus Christ. If money is such a strong pull you are absorbed in the cares of this life, then bridal love is on a separate plane than you. Money is a joke in the face of this bridal love. The bible is clear that man cannot serve two masters (Matthew 6:24). Meaning that money really carries weight in the hearts of people. 1 Timothy 6:10 says, "For the love of money is the root of all kinds of evil."

True bridal love dominates the pull and power of wealth. It's simply a different type of love and on a different calibur. Why is wealth listed last? Because if someone said to you, "I will give you a million dollars or death," obviously *death* would be the last one you would choose. As a result, the bride comes right out the gate declaring that love is stronger than death. We know God is into us being blessed and prospering and being in good health. Yet with true bridal love there is no price that will allow you to sell your soul. They are just wasting their time trying. We need to invest our lives into this type of love because it's the most valuable thing on this side of heaven.

14. INGREDIENTS OF THE BRIDAL COMPANY: OBEDIENCE

Obedience is the last attribute that marks the bride. *Obedience is radical abandonment in complete surrender.* Jesus says, "If you love me, you will obey my commands" (John 14:15). The first and greatest command is to love Him with all your heart, soul, and mind. But then onto the second command, which Jesus said is likened unto the first. There is great weight in loving our neighbor. We also have the great commission. This is not the great suggestion—it was a command. He commanded us to go preach the gospel, heal the sick, cast out devils, and raise the dead. James even mentioned later on that looking after widows and orphans is the true religion. Obedience is to go about these works.

Obedience looks like so many different things and if we are not careful sometimes, we can get so top heavy in the lingo of love and that there is no fruit in obedience. Jesus said, "If you love me you will obey my commands," *plural* not just the one of loving Him. If you truly love Him then by default the other commands will fall into place. We have to stay full and balanced in the word. Don't get me wrong, there will be seasons where the Lord will lock you up to just be with Him. The 'go' of the gospel comes later. He first called the disciples to be with Him and then he sent them out.

The bridal company is full of radical abandonment and complete obedience to the bridegroom. The *depth* at which you truly love will always be in direct reflection to the *accuracy* in which you obey. Many talk a big love game but the fruit is always seen in their obedience.

I long for us to be yielding people, moldable people. May we be like clay in his hands. The bride is pure, spotless burning with fiery unquenchable love. The waters of this world can't put it out. It burns too bright, even brighter than death and greater than persecution. I can say 'no thanks' to wealth if it tries to buy me off from my first infatuated love as a seal on his heart and arm. The riches of this world look like monopoly money compared to bridal love.

Love and obedience go hand in hand

The bridal realm cannot be bought. You'd think the bridal company is crazy if you look at them from the world's point of view. Sometimes if we are not careful, we can even put the time into the secret place but if we are not yielded out of obedience something is not right. The bible says wisdom proves itself by its fruit (Luke 7:35). You can look at the fruit of any tree if you want to see it's fruit. Obedience is the result of love. I'm not trying to point fingers but that we may evaluate our own lives and ask Jesus to help us to love Him more purely so that there would be fruit. Love and obedience are inseparable.

The quality of your obedience will show you the condition of your love. Many people can go into prayer, which I suggest we do more of, but again if the obedience isn't matching, we can have the glory of God in our corporate meetings but then He tells us to do one little thing and we draw back. The bride does not put her will and desires over His. The bride is one hundred percent yielded, completely pliable and full of humility. When Jesus says, "Jump." the bride says, "How high?" You can see a maturity in our love in our ability to obey—*and* how quickly and thoroughly we obey. The two are inseparable.

If your obedience is sketchy at times then you need to go deeper in bridal love. "His pleasure," referring to Jesus, "is the bride's greatest desire and fulfilling His wishes is the most important thing to her." The bride loves Him so much that she just wants to obey rightly. The bridal company is and will always be marked by unmatched capacity to obey.

In Ephesians 5, Paul talks about the submission of the wife to the husband and compares it to Christ and the church. Jesus exemplified a life of yielding to the Father. "Not My will but Your will be done." He was led like a lamb to the slaughter. Likewise, we are to submit ourselves to Jesus wholly and completely. I have heard it said that delayed obedience is disobedience. I remember Bobby Conner was once asked, "What is the most important thing one could do in their Christian life?" He quickly said, "To obey." This is produced from rich, bridal love.

15. BRIDAL UNION

"The Spirit and the bride say, "Come." And let the one who hears say, "Come." And let the one who is thirsty come; let the one who wishes take the water of life without cost." (Revelation 22:17)

You will notice in the verse above, there are three different companies in the context of the return of the Lord. The book of revelation is very unique in itself because it's not written in chronological order. The chapters of Revelation are overlapping and scholars will attest to this. So basically you have John writing this encounter and in some of the chapters the Lord has already returned and has already begun to become one with His bride and has had the wedding feast.

In revelation 22, He closes the book and John is back in real time and the Lord has not returned yet. Here you see these three different companies. We must emphasize the eternal over *natural* marriage though I am huge on natural marriage. The return of the Lord and union with Him is the focal point of eternity in our marriage to Him. In this place even natural marriage disappears.

The passage says, as we've quoted, "The Spirit and the Bride say come." Out of the gate you see the Spirit, the Holy Spirit mentioned. Prior to Christ's return the Holy Spirit is active on earth. He is God, at work among us. He was sent on the day of pentecost and is behind all the activity of the kingdom. So, that tells us, the Bride is formed even before the coming of the Lord. One thing you notice is that the Spirit and the Bride are one in Revelation 22:17. There is no separation between the church and the Holy Spirit. We know from scripture that the Holy Spirit is the seal. There is a company marked by unity that is called the Bride before the coming of the Lord.

This company is one with the Spirit and are together crying, "Come Lord." The rest of the verse then mentions a different company. It says, "and the one who hears says, 'come.'" It's meant to join two separate things like peanut butter and jelly, sheep and goats, the wheat and the tare. The Holy Spirit longs for the consummation of all things. They are saying come together, the Spirit and the Bride. The Bride and the Spirit saying come is just what they do, they don't know anything else but to beckon Jesus to come because of their deep love for the bridegroom.

How to measure where you are spiritually

One of the ways you can measure where you are spiritually is if there's a constant yearning in your heart that Jesus would come. Not necessarily in reference to his coming, but there should be a longing to be with Him in intimacy and union. The bridal company is always desperate for Him to come, that's just the cry of their heart. The bridal company doesn't see anything else—they are brainwashed and infatuated with Jesus Christ. They are the most yielded one and bear the most fruit.

The bride says, "Come," from the secret place. The second company comes from, "Let those who hear say, "come." With this company there is a reminder given and it's more *advisory*. The third company says, "Let he who is thirsty come." This one is totally different. "Come," is not even mentioned and they are all titled differently in the context of the return of the Lord. John is writing about three companies that are completely infatuated with Jesus.

As I have traveled around the world and been around different streams and circles, I have noticed something. You can hear in the tone of a person's voice whether they are just working and doing ministry or whether they are possessed by love and infatuation. I am not trying to be an inspector gadget on it but you can just hear it in people's voices and tone.

The first company has a deeper intimacy with Jesus and they don't need to be told to say, "Come." The second company has a lesser relationship, they have to be told and reminded to say, "Come." The third company is told, "Let those that are thirsty come." These are those who are not born again. John is basically making a broad appeal that touches everybody.

All the others that are saved are to cry, "Come, Lord," yet the last company is not told to say this. They are told to come to the Lord first. The last company can not say *come* because they themselves must first come to the waters of life and drink of salvation. There is no good thing awaiting those that say, "Come, Lord Jesus," if they are not born again but eternally burning in the lake of fire and judgment.

Characteristics of the Bridal Company in Union with Christ

My desire for you and me is that we would be in the bridal company, the first company crying with the spirit in union for Jesus to come. You basically want your secret place life to look like the first company which is a deep burning love and infatuation for Jesus where you have hoarded oil out of intimacy in which there is no routine but deep yearning to be with the bridegroom. As leaders it's important that we keep pulling the people back to that place of intimacy. Because there is a difference on the other side of glory for those who are the yielded ones. In the company those that hear is a more general company of believers. If you are not saved you don't say hear this company is saved and that's why John says let them say come. Which means in the heart of this company it's not a natural desire to say come because John has to instruct or remind them to do so. It doesn't burn in them like the first company.

If you are not born again, you are thirsty. This is why as an unbeliever you have to drink from all these various places—and even then you aren't satisfied. In this world, there is a lot of false water. In John 4 Jesus talks to the Samaritan woman using the illustration of water. He tells the women to get this living water. He then says that those who drink of the water that Jesus gives will never thirst again.

The scriptures regularly speak of the father-son relationship we have with God. This is deep, but not as deep as husband and wife. This is a broad encounter he wants us to dig into out of a place of hunger. Jesus spoke in parables for us to search them out in His glory. The scriptures say, "He who overcomes shall inherit all things, and I will be his God and he shall be My son. But the cowardly, unbelieving, abominable, murderers, sexually immoral, sorcerers, idolaters, and all liars shall have their part in the lake which burns with fire and brimstone, which is the second death" (Revelation 21:8).

This is the word. There is a real hell. Don't heed those that say there is no hell. It is all over the Word. The lost experience eternal damnation, yet we don't have to go there. We can, indeed, experience life everlasting. While I so honor and love the fact that the scripture is filled with references to us being in a father-son relationship with

God, I also see that there is something deeper. That something deeper is a husband-wife relationship with God.

One of the seven angels came to John and said, "Let me show you the bride, the wife of the lamb." John said, "He carried me to a mountain and showed me the Holy city Jerusalem coming down from God." The bridal company is possessed. They have touched the very heart of God. Nothing else will do with this company of people. They are completely in love.

We need to cry out for the return of the Lord in our everyday secret place in life. We should cry out for that daily bread—the fresh manna and oil of the Lord. Jesus, our bridegroom, is raising up his bridal company that goes beyond church as usual. Through his word, the Bridegroom has given us our bridal assignments from a place of intimacy.

My prayer is that our lives would embody all of these ingredients, the purity, the deep love that then produces quick and thorough obedience. May we allow the Lord to take precedence in our lives and cloak us in his closeness. As the bride of Christ, may we ask ourselves, "Have I made myself ready to be a part of the Bridegroom's last day bridal company?"

ABOUT THE AUTHOR

BRIAN GUERIN is the founding president of Bridal Glory International. He graduated from the Brownsville School of Ministry/F.I.R.E. in 2001, and now travels throughout the U.S. and the world teaching and preaching the gospel of the Lord Jesus Christ. Brian has appeared on T.B.N. and GOD-TV and currently hosts his own broadcasting channel on YouTube. He also authored two previously released books, *Modern Day Mysticism* and *God of Wonders*. His main passion and emphasis in life is to draw the Bride of Christ into greater intimacy with the Bridegroom Himself-Jesus Christ, leading to the maturity of the Bride and the culmination of His glorious return. Brian also enjoys bringing great emphasis and depth to the art of hearing the voice of God through dreams, visions, signs, and wonders.

VISIT BRIDAL GLORY ON THE WEB & SOCIAL:
WWW.BRIDALGLORY.COM

SOCIAL: @BRIDALGLORY

FREE EXCERPT FROM
CONTEMPLATIONS ON **CHARACTER**

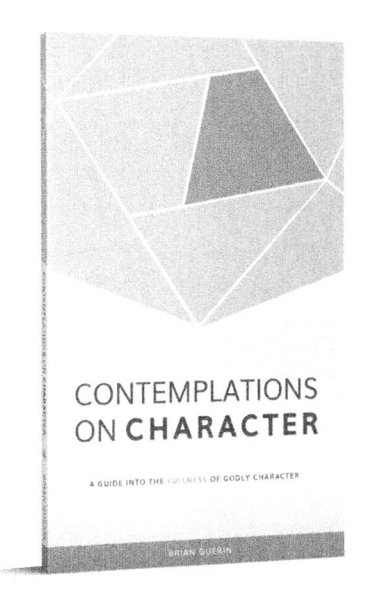

CONTEMPLATIONS ON **CHARACTER**

A GUIDE INTO THE FULLNESS OF GODLY CHARACTER

BRIAN GUERIN

AVAILABLE AT
amazon

CHAPTER ONE
A CASE FOR CHARACTER

If you've attended our schools, read our books or followed our ministry, it won't take you long to realize that we love the supernatural, the anointing and the gifts of the Spirit. Having said that, we are called to exemplify the person of Jesus Christ in *every* facet of His nature, leaving nothing out.

As a result, the topic of godly character cannot be omitted from our ministries. When you look at the dark spiral of society we are seeing a need for purity and a "called out" godliness like never before. I pray that through this work we see massive differences in our individual lives, our ministries, our marriages, and our personas as a whole.

When tackling the topic of character, I've heard things like, "Character? That's not a topic many will be drawn to." Yet we ought to be drawn to *all things Jesus*...and the topic of character is at the center of Christ's heart. Anointing, gifting, and knowledge of the Word cannot supplant character nor is an emphasis on character to eliminate the supernatural. You'll actually discover that godly character is indeed *supernatural*. Walking in integrity is just as supernatural as prophesying. Putting the grocery basket back where you found it can be just as godly as laying hands on the sick.

Throughout this book I will be bringing to light several

areas of God's character and we will unpack the implications of that character in our own lives. It should go without saying but as we do, it's by no means meant to be condemning or judgmental. Perhaps you have failed in some of these areas of character. I can tell you I've failed in all of these areas. Teaching on character is by no means driven by guilt, condemnation or shame, but instead is intended to stir us up and encourage us to take on God's attributes more and more each day.

I pray that through this book you are brought into new measures and revelations of the rock-solid character of God and as a result, let His character become one with yours. As you grow in His nature and likeness, may you be well prepared to steward all that He would have for you today, tomorrow, and forever.

CHAPTER TWO
INFRASTRUCTURE

Character (noun): the mental and moral makeup of an individual.

The ultimate goal of life is to know God and, from that place, to reflect His likeness. Yet we are incapable of exuding a character and a moral standard that we ourselves have not been exposed to. Throughout the scripture we see the value of seeking Jesus and catching a revelation of who He is, that we might reflect His very nature. I believe in the simplicity of the gospel. I truly believe that by simply yielding to Jesus, everything else will fall into place. You can spend some time in the privacy of a prayer closet and be molded into the image of Jesus far more than reading countless self-help guides.

Yet at the same time, we see that examples of God's nature can also be found in *people*. Not only can it be *found* in people, but it can be *honored* and *duplicated* by us. In fact, Paul made some incredible statements about character and imitation in his letters to the Corinthians.

> "Imitate me, just as I also imitate Christ." (1 Corinthians 11:1)

> "Therefore I urge you, imitate me. For this reason I have sent Timothy to you, who is my beloved and faithful son in the Lord, who will remind you of my ways in Christ, as I teach everywhere in every church." (1 Corinthians 4:16-17).

With the risk of sounding arrogant, Paul implores the church to follow him. Why? Because he knew that he was pulling from the character of God and if they looked to that example, a trickle down effect would manifest. Notice, Paul said, "My son in the faith, Timothy, will remind you of my *ways*." What are Paul's "ways"? His character. He had so allowed God's character to superimpose his, that he was comfortable putting himself out there as a tangible model for what godliness would look like in the church. To the Ephesians he expressed similar sentiments:

"Therefore be imitators of God as dear children. And walk in love, as Christ also has loved us and given Himself for us, an offering and a sacrifice to God for a sweet-smelling aroma." (Ephesians 5:1-2)

The Greek definition of *imitate* here means to mimic, emulate, mirror, echo or reproduce. I find it interesting that he told the church to imitate God. In other words, it's a conscious choice to begin shaping your ways to match God's.

"We shall be like Him, for we shall see Him as He is." (1 John 3:2)

Of course this passage will take place at Christ's return but there is also a prophetic blueprint showing us how Christlikeness occurs—by and through beholding Him. In doing so, His temperament, personality, way of speaking, and way of responding is automatically adopted by us. This can be a long process or a slow process of development but I do believe these things can be accelerated through the access we have as New Testament believers.

"But we all, with unveiled face, beholding as in a mirror the glory of the Lord, are being transformed into the same image from glory to glory, just as by the Spirit of the Lord." (2 Corinthians 3:18)

Again, the emphasis of Paul is for Christ's church to

look like Christ Himself. If we are honest, as humans we are naturally wired to to yield in certain areas whereas other areas might be more difficult. For example, some of us are naturally more easygoing and patient. As a result, those traits come easy. Yet we might struggle more with self-discipline, for example. Whereas some may have no problem with something like unforgiveness, but might struggle with self-pity. Needless to say, no matter what our natural tendencies are, God has called us to be full and mature in Christ, leaving no area unchecked. When He has our gaze, these things happen with ease compared to trying varied methods of behavior modification.

We've all seen it, you become like those you spend time with. Have you ever become close with a new group of friends and suddenly, you begin talking like them? You might even start laughing like them and walking like them. This can be dangerous if you are running with the wrong crowd. Yet when you're spending time with Christ and with people who imitate Christ, you'll begin to imitate a godly example, thereby producing godly fruit.

"For I am the Lord, I do not change." (Malachi 3:6)

"Jesus Christ is the same yesterday, today, and forever." (Hebrews 13:8)

Let's face it, it's hard to hit a moving target. If God were always changing, it would be nearly impossible to become like Him. The second you began to emulate Him, He would change His ways and you would no longer be like Him. The fact that He remains consistently steady allows us to aim at His example and to *attain* His example. Knowing that God remains the same is a stabilizing and securing element on our end relationally. We know He is not going to respond to something a certain way today and then totally change His being and respond differently tomorrow. We are able to rest in His consistency.

I've come to see that the people that reflect His character and likeness in a full way, stay the same over the years. In other words, they are not on a rollercoaster with fluctuating character and an oscillating personality. This doesn't mean that anyone stops growing. What it *does* mean is that there is a steadiness that keeps a character-filled believer from living from valley to mountain peak and back down to the valley again.

We even see James describe God with unique language in his epistle, "Every good gift and every perfect gift is from above, and comes down from the Father of lights, with whom there is no variation or shadow of turning" (James 1:17). There is no variation with God. When you see people walk with Jesus for a long period of time, you see them experience punches from life. When that happens, you get a feel for whether or not there is "variation" in them. Those who genuinely walk in God's character have a stability that causes them to respond with grace both in good times, and bad.

A HEAVENLY ALIGNMENT

Jesus said, "Therefore you shall be perfect, just as your Father in heaven is perfect" (Matthew 5:48). Yet we also see the scriptures say, "If we say that we have no sin, we deceive ourselves, and the truth is not in us" (1 John 1:8). So what do we make of this? We must live with a balanced mindset that is subject to the full and complete lens of scripture. Yet we also must realize the standard that Jesus has called us to live out. The word *perfect* that Jesus used is actually the Greek word for *mature*. God is wanting to elevate our character to a place of maturity and fullness.

I was recently talking to a friend of mine who said he had spent time with a ministry of true acclaim and notoriety. This minister had experienced incredible prophetic visitations and was used mightily in the anointing. Yet my friend and this minister hopped in a taxi together and when the driver wasn't getting them where they needed to be, character seemed to go out the window in terms of responses and behavior. Rudeness and impatience was unashamedly displayed toward the driver by this particular minister. Point being, visitations and being used of God will not insulate you from the need to walk in godly character. A lifetime of mighty ministry can be thrown out with a short burst of character compromise. The world won't necessarily be impressed with our ministries, but they will be impressed with our integrity!

Coming into alignment with God's will for our maturity can happen rapidly when we *yield*. Of course, we can go around the wilderness for 40 years when it ought to be an 11 day journey, but God's desire is *acceleration*. Acceleration is not necessarily taking shortcuts, but rather leveraging our position in Christ will cause *character acceleration* and a rapid development into the image of Jesus.

CHAPTER THREE
CHOICES AND FEELINGS

As we build the topic of this book, I want to make it clear: character has nothing to do with *feelings*. It can *incorporate* feelings but it's never *driven* by them. When you mirror God, it may cause good feelings in you—but it's not the determining factor of them. In the forthcoming chapters we will take a deep look at dozens of aspects of character. As we do, it's quite easy to only walk in them when we *feel like it*. Yet God gave us no feeling-based contingency in the word. Right is right, whether feelings agree or not.

> "But above all these things put on love, which is the bond of perfection. And let the peace of God rule in your hearts, to which also you were called in one body; and be thankful." (Colossians 3:14-15)

Notice, he says that *we* must put on love. That's a choice. It doesn't say that love will overtake us but that we choose to pick it up and put it on. In this case, God won't do for you what you must do for you. It's sort of like how at a certain age, you require your children to tie their own shoes. Otherwise, you would be hindering them by doing everything for them. Now, you might guide them, remind them of the how-to's and what the bunny ears should look like. But they are still doing the tying. Likewise, God requires us to put things on and put things off in the spirit. We aren't far from His help, guidance, and encouragement. Yet effort is required on our part.

All of this is available and forever opened to the people of God through Christ's death and resurrection. It is a treasury room that has been broken open. Yet you have to activate your hands and feet, walk in and grab it. You'll find as you grow and mature in the things of God it is no longer like pulling teeth to put on love. Instead, it's a joy. It's not that you *have* to walk in love and kindness but that you *get* to.

The longer you submit to your feelings as the driving force of your life, the harder it is to get out of it. Those who have been steeped in feeling and emotion-based decision making for decades, might struggle to break these cycles. This is why the Bible talks about refusing to let the sun go down on your wrath. I tell my kids, "Get off of the wave." What that means is when life happens, hurts take place, expectations are failed, and these feelings carry you—they start to build up like a wave and if you don't get off early, you get trapped in it and end up crashing with it.

Sometimes women get a bad rap, accused of making decisions by emotions and feelings, but no doubt men can be absolute emotional rollercoasters as well. It's not gender specific. It's for all to grasp. Often we let cultural norms steal from our fruit. Because of circumstances, events that take place, or the way we are treated—we let our demeanor be taken over by fruit that didn't come from God. The more you cling to the Holy Spirit, the easier it becomes to recognize that those characteristics don't belong. You become quick to cut off rotten fruit from growing in you.

You see, we were not given the right to operate in any other fruit. Our characteristics are to come from the fruit of the Spirit we see in Galatians 5. If it doesn't come from the fruit of the Spirit, then weeds will grow, Ishmaels will be produced and ugly stuff will sprout in the garden of our lives.

Feelings are a great benefit of life. I love the feeling of catching a fish or having a great coffee. But these things are merely a benefactor of the choices we make in life. They are God-given *contributors* to the makeup of humanity, but they were never intended to be the driving force of our lives. Many live by *feelings*...when *faith* is to be our mainstay. As we examine the high standard God has called us to in the coming chapters, keep in mind that the agreement of your feelings is not required. Simply yielding to the Holy Spirit and the example of Christ will cause seemingly unattainable character to be the very character you display.

*ENTIRE BOOK CAN BE PURCHASED IN **PAPERBACK** AND **EBOOK** FORMATS ON **AMAZON.COM**

NOTES

Notes

Notes

Notes

Notes

Notes

Notes

Notes

Notes

Notes

Printed in Great Britain
by Amazon